99
thoughts
about
girls

for guys' eyes only

insights to what teenage girls are really like

a book for guys
by katie edwards
with kurt johnston

99 Thoughts About Girls: For Guys' Eyes Only
Copyright © 2009 Simply Youth Ministry

Simply Youth Ministry
26981 Vista Terrace, Unit C
Lake Forest, CA 92630

www.simplyyouthministry.com
www.simplyjuniorhigh.com

ISBN 978-0-7644-6232-0

Printed in the United States of America

about katie edwards

Katie Edwards has been involved in junior high ministry for more than 15 years, and is currently serving at Saddleback Church in Southern California. She has a passion for helping teenagers grow in their relationship with Jesus and equipping them to make wise choices. Katie enjoys life with her husband, Ron, and their daughter, Abby Jane.

about kurt johnston

Kurt Johnston has been working in junior high ministry since 1988 and right now is the junior high pastor at Saddleback Church. He loves providing resources for junior high ministry almost as much as he loves junior highers themselves. Kurt loves surfing, dirt bike riding, and hanging out with his family.

99 thoughts about girls: for guys' eyes only

table of contents

a note from katie:

You are about to enter the unknown...the world of girls.

Wow, you are brave. Any boy who takes steps to better understand girls is a hero in my book. Not that you can ever fully understand them. I say this because girls are unique creatures with layers and layers of complex emotions and actions. They can love you one minute and hate you the next. They don't need a reason, they're girls and that is enough. No two girls are alike, and because of this fact I am not sure any book could accurately tell you everything you need to know about them. Arguably, one girl often has multiple personalities, so even this book might totally apply one minute and should be thrown out the next. However, be encouraged – there are some thoughts in this book that I think can help guide you on your journey to better understanding and existing in the world of girls. I am hoping you will gain some small insight into being friends with girls, asking girls out, dating girls, and avoiding certain areas and topics when around girls.

comment from kurt

She's right, guys. I've been married to my wife for almost 20 years and I'm still trying to figure her out! But that's part of what makes them so special; if they were just like us, they wouldn't be very interesting, would they?

An important fact to remember as you read this book is that God is the master creator and He made of each us to be unique and special. In light of this fact, this book is not describing every girl at every moment in her life. It's simply a collection of thoughts and tips to give you a small glimpse into the world of girls. Each girl you meet is an individual who is feeling individual emotions, jumping over individual obstacles, and figuring out her individual journey.

My hope is that this book will give you some words of wisdom to help you understand us just a little bit better and hopefully set you on the road to healthy, lifelong friendships and relationships with the girls God brings into your life.

Katie

Katie Edwards

the world of girls

1. Girls are SOOOOO different than you.

It's true – guys and girls are extremely different from one another. We look different, we talk different, we think different, we see the world differently, we smell differently...I guess you get the idea! But the differences between us are not a bad thing! It's actually kind of fun. Can you imagine how boring relationships would be if we were too similar? Even though there is a lot to learn about girls, the journey of spending time with them and figuring them out can be super fun. Think of girls as a mystery that can be solved if you work hard solving the case. Good luck with that, Sherlock!

2. Girls are wonderfully complex.

You may think that at some point in your life you will be able to fully understand girls. Unfortunately that day may never come. Girls are complex. They have lots of layers that make up who they are. This may sound discouraging, but really it is one of the coolest things about girls. They are never boring and will always keep you guessing. They are deep, fascinating, and full of surprises. Join the legions of men that throughout history have tried to figure out girls – just embrace it or die trying.

3. God created girls the way they are for a reason.

Girls can sometimes seem like a mystery, but they were created to exist with you! God made girls with all of their differences, emotions, and attributes to be a partner and a companion to you. This uniqueness not only makes them great partners, but they were created with their differences so that God could use them in ways that are unique only to the ladies! You may not always be able to figure them out, but you can enjoy them for who God made them to be.

4. Girls are looking for **love and acceptance.**

Girls are searching. They are searching for people who will love and accept them just as they are. More than anything girls want to surround themselves with people who want to know them, care about them, and love them. It is important that you know this because this small fact influences just about everything in the life of a girl.

comment from kurt

Guys, when you think about it, everybody wants to be loved and accepted. One of the greatest gifts you could ever give a girl is the simple gift of friendship and acceptance with no strings attached.

most of the time, sometimes, or always

Unfortunately for you, no two girls are alike. As I said before they are complex and unpredictable. You will sometimes – well, most of the time or always – catch certain things to be true about girls.

5. Most of the time girls think this planet revolves solely around them. It does, but only in their minds.

Girls enter into each day believing that everyone and everything is simply existing in their world. It sounds self-absorbed, but really it isn't. It is just the fact that girls tackle the day thinking about how everyone around them will respond to who they are.

6. Sometimes girls cry for no reason.

There are times when girls are emotional for no reason. It could be triggered by a movie or by a commerical. It could be a cute puppy they just saw or a memory from long ago about a puppy in a kennel that triggers tears. If you ask them what's wrong, they will respond with an "I'm fine" or "Nothing." This really can't be explained in rational terms. Try not to stare. Just let it happen.

comment from kurt

Guys, this is what we're tempted to say sometimes...
1. "Seriously? Get over it!" 2. "What are you, some sort of sissy?" 3. "Oh no...here we go again!" (And roll your eyes for an added bonus.)
I have said these things to my teenage daughter. Not good.

7. Girls are **always comparing** themselves to someone or something.

In girl world, it is safe to assume that comparison is the name of the game. Girls compare themselves to other girls about everything! Body types, clothes, metabolism, hair style, breath, grades, size of bedroom...you name it, they've compared it already.

8. Most of the time girls **think about their outfit** for the next day the night before.

(This is a weird fact but one that will help you understand the process of a girl preparing for the day.) Girls lie in bed the night before and think about the outfit they are going to wear the next day. This is an exhaustive process of elimination that needs to take place before we can get ready. There are a few things that factor into an outfit decision:

4

- Who will see the outfit? (If this is a cute outfit – maximum people need to see it.)
- What activities will be happening throughout the day? (Busy schedule, PE 4th period, or going on an after-school outing.)
- What is happening the rest of the week? Do I need to save a certain outfit for later in the week? (Possible encounter with a crush on Thursday – this is cause to save the perfect pair of jeans for later in the week.)

Choosing what to wear on any given day is a total process; you have no idea how this works because lots of guys pick up clothes off the floor, smell them, and put on whatever doesn't make them wince. There is no exaggeration in this statement – I know adult men who still do this.

9. Girls are **always emotional.**

Our emotions rule us. And at any given time they could rule you too. We tend to let our emotions and feelings guide our decisions and actions. And for the most part we aren't afraid to let our emotions show. We can be joyous and outgoing one minute and then two seconds later we can be heartbroken and sad. Our emotions are present in everything we do. The way we feel affects everything we are and everything we do. Even writing this paragraph makes me want to laugh and cry at the same time. See what I mean?

10. Most of the time you don't see **all of a girl** on the surface.

There are layers to every girl and she chooses when to reveal those layers to you. Girls naturally hide things about themselves in order to protect themselves from getting hurt. The more time you take to get to know a girl, the more she will reveal about her true self. Time, love, and genuineness will allow you to peek inside and see who she really is. When you break that trust, you have to start all over again.

comment from kurt

I know that we guys tend to focus on the outward appearance of a girl. If she's cute, we like her! By judging girls solely on their outward appearance, we are being really unfair to them. Try to be different than most guys and be willing to look below the surface, too.

11. Sometimes the littlest things **can ruin a girl's whole day.**

A bad hair day, a bad grade, a stain on her shirt, a bird pooping on their head, a teacher yelling at them, a friend making fun of them – something little like this could alter a girl's state of mind for the whole day. And sometimes there is

6

no chance to recover until a new day begins. Sleep is the girl's natural defense.

12. Most of the time there is **strength in numbers.**

Ever wonder why girls go to the bathroom together or why we stand in little huddles or why we walk with our arms linked? One reason: There is total strength and security in numbers. We love to be surrounded by our close friends in any given situation. Somehow, it gives us a sense of total support when facing boys, other girls, school, and – believe it or not – the bathroom.

comment from kurt

Okay, I guess that makes sense. But seriously, 13 girls going to the bathroom together is still kinda weird!

13. Girls sometimes make decisions based on **the way they feel.**

There are times when we girls make decisions according to logic. However, there are also times when we make decisions based on pure emotion and feeling. Happy, sad, melancholy – any of these feelings could make a decision for us. How we feel can heavily play into the outcome of a situation or a choice we make. We think with our hearts, not with our heads. You must never use that to your advantage. Understand?

14. Most of the time **how we feel physically** affects the way we treat others.

Teenage girls have hormones. Sometimes those hormones can be in control of our brain and our mouth. If you find yourself in a situation like this, just speak in a gentle tone and nod your head a lot; you can't really do anything right when a girl is in a hormonal state – sorry. Listening is your best defense on this one. Being a good listener always wins.

15. Sometimes we will try to reject you **before you reject us.**

Getting rejected by a girl friend or a guy friend is one of the worst things a girl can experience. It snowballs out of control through the school and usually the hot information even beats them home. If girls catch even a hint of rejection coming their way, they automatically look for ways to save face and reject you first. I think it is a God-given instinct that all girls are born with. Someone once called it "rejection-phobia."

For example: A girl texts you and asks if you want to come to her birthday party. You can't go because of football practice. You tell one of her friends who got invited that you can't go. The friend tells the girl. The girl is bummed. And before she sees you, she will figure out some way to reject you first before you even get the chance to tell her firsthand that you cannot come because of a previous commitment. So when you finally see each other she will say something like, "Oh, well, I invited tons of guys – so it's really not that big of a deal that you aren't going to be there." Or she might say, "It's no big deal that you can't come. I just invited you because I didn't want you to feel left out." Confusing, right? The thought of rejection can be powerful, and if there is anyway to avoid rejection, girls will do it.

being a guy in girl world

It's a girl's world. At least that's the way we see it. It's important for you to learn how to exist in the world of girls.

16. Be nice.
Girls love to hang out with nice guys. They might not always want to date nice guys, but girls really like spending time and being around nice guys. The nice guy always gets the girl ... unfortunately, sometimes the girl has to get burned by the bad guy first.

17. Do not embarrass her in front of others.
Girls HATE being embarrassed by guys – especially if it happens in front of others. We like to joke around and we like teasing, but teasing can easily go too far and turn into humiliation and embarrassment. You might as well shoot us. Just be aware and try to control how far you take something; it'll be remembered for a long time.

comment from kurt

Guys, I think what Katie means is don't embarrass a girl ON PURPOSE. There's no doubt you will embarrass her by accident just because you're a guy and you can be kinda embarrassing without even trying!

18. Clean yourself up a little bit – girls like a guy who **takes care of himself.**

Girls love guys who take showers, smell nice, and look presentable. You don't have to be wearing a suit or be super stylish – you just need to wear clean clothes and look like you care a little about your appearance. We really don't like greasy hair and dirty, smelly clothes – yuck.

comment from kurt

This one is TOTALLY true. I wish it wasn't because I like being sloppy.

19. Be a talker...**but not too much.**

Girls like to talk. They really like when guys can carry on a conversation. Ask her questions. Talk about yourself a little. But be careful – don't get too carried away and dominate the conversation so she can't get a word in.

10

You don't want the girl to think you are the "freaky talker guy" who won't shut up.

20. Be **yourself.**
Don't try to become what you think WE want you to be. Be honest about who you are and let us see what you are really about. We really just want to know the real you. And if you act fake or try to be something you are not, eventually we will find out and we will be bummed that you lied about who you were. Be you and it will save us all a lot of time.

21. Watch **your mouth.**
You may think swearing and talking dirty is super funny, and maybe it flies with your guy friends – but ultimately it is a turnoff for girls. Sure, we might stand in the circle and laugh at you – but it won't get you closer to us and we certainly would be cautious about having a serious conversation with you. Using words that target girls are never winners with girls.

22. Be **friendly to those around her.**
Girls like it when you are nice to the people she loves, such as her mom, her best friends, or her little sister. A girl is more likely to invite you places or hang out with you more if you get along well with the other people in her life. Plus, no matter what she says, their opinion of you matters to her almost as much as her own.

23. Be sensitive.

Remember girls are all about feelings. So, when you hear the story about her dog's broken paw or the "D" on her test, be sensitive to how she feels. Even though something might not seem like a big deal to you, it could be a big deal to her. Hear her out and be there for her. You don't need to do anything.

comment from kurt

Guys, this may be one of the most important things you will ever learn about girls. Your willingness to listen and pay attention when a girl is sharing her feelings is one of the best ways to show her that you really care about your friendship. My wife was reminding me of this the other night, but I forget what she said because I wasn't listening.

24. Let a girl be the center of attention without making her the center of attention.

Girls like attention – but they don't always like attention being drawn to them. They like for you to notice the outfit they are wearing or that they got a haircut – but they don't necessarily want you to yell that across the room.

25. Don't lie to us.

We HATE being lied to. As often as possible be honest, even if the truth is tough to hear. When we are lied to or betrayed we have a tough time with forgiveness. You will also soon learn that you can only burn a girl so many times. If you think elephants have a long memory, wait until you experience ours. You might have difficulty rebuilding trust with a girl you have lied to.

being friends with a girl

Girls love their friends. In fact, friendships are one of the most important things in a girl's life. And those are friendships with guy and girls. If you can learn to get past the awkward guy/girl thing, you might just find out that girls can be some of the closest friends you have.

26. Be genuine.
If you really want to be friends with a girl, then act like a real friend. Care about her as a person and not as a potential girl to date. Be real and true in your friendship motives. Girls are looking for friends who truly want to be there for them.

27. Be a listener, not a fixer.
Sometimes girls just need a friend to listen about the things happening in their life. They don't need you to fix anything or solve the problem for them (which can be difficult for guys, because you are often looking to be the hero when around your girl friends). Everything in your body will make you want to fix it, probably with your fists. You must resist the urge to

"fix it," and just listen. You can offer up advice at times – but most of the time girls just want someone who will sit by them and be on their side.

28. Give her **compliments.**

Girls really love compliments! They love when guys take the time to notice things about them. It is a surefire way to make a girl's day. Side note: Don't make things up – we totally know when you are doing it, and it sucks.

29. Accept her for **who she is.**

Don't try to change her or expect her to be something that she is not. Love her for who she is. Girls like it when friends accept them at their very best and at their very worst. Acceptance means accepting the whole package – annoying habits and all.

30. Don't let your friendship **become all about her.**

Your friendship should be give and take. A "girl" friend should care about you and your interests as much as you care about her and her interests. Don't let a girl get away with not being a good friend to you in return. You deserve good friends in your life who care about the real you. Even if that includes Star Wars and Monday Night Football.

comment from kurt

This is really hard to do if you think the girl is cute or you are hoping to become more than "just friends." But, unfortunately some girls will take advantage of you and abuse your friendship if you let them.

31. Cheer **her on.**

Encouragement is key in any friendship. It feels great to have your friends in your corner cheering you on. When your girl friends are trying out for the basketball team or they did well on a really big test – cheer them on. Give them a huge pat on the back or "way to go."

32. Remember **things.**

This one kind of goes hand in hand with being a good listener. When a girl tells you something – remember. Girls hate it when you ask them the same question six times or forget an important date that matters to them.

33. Hang out **in groups.**

When you truly want to be a friend to a girl, remove any kind of goofy dating pressure by hanging out in a group of friends instead of one on one. In a group, you can spend time together and know each other on a deeper level without any relationship weirdness getting in the way.

34. Keep your flirting **under control.**

It is pretty natural for guys and girls to flirt. Even if you are just friends, flirting can take place. Be aware of this fact and try to keep it under control. The more comfortable you get with a girl the easier it gets to start flirting, but be careful because she can turn the corner towards liking you quicker than you will. Before you know it she has planned your wedding.

comment from kurt

Guys, flirting is especially dangerous when you know the girl likes you but you don't like her back. Flirting sends all kinds of signals, and it's not a good idea to purposely send the wrong signals to somebody.

35. Girl friends are **not like your guy friends.**

Seriously – they are not even close to your guy friends. Don't tease them like you tease your guys friends, don't talk to them the way you talk to your guy friends, don't punch them in the arm the way you punch your guy friends in the arm – just don't. They are different. Go back to the beginning of this book and re-read everything as a reminder for how to treat your girl friends.

comment from kurt

Girls take teasing totally differently than guys do. You can't joke around and tease girls the same way you do with your buddies. Sadly, you won't learn just from reading this. Like all other men before you, you will learn the hard way!

36. Friendships **take time.**

Real friendships are built over time. Don't expect to get to know a girl in a week. It will take you a while to feel like you really know a girl friend well. The more time you spend together, the more she will reveal about herself.

37. Balance your **friendships.**

Your guy friends should get the same kind of attention as your girl friends. Girl world can be exciting at times and you might feel the urge to leave guy friends behind; don't do that. Spend equal amounts of time with your guy and girl friends – and combine when possible. Don't abandon dude friends; balance it out. Side note: If you feel like you want to spend all of your time with one girl friend, you have turned the "I totally want to date this girl and not be just friends with her" corner.

38. Finding friends who love God **is not a bad idea.**

Look for girl friends who love God. Finding friends who are like-minded with you when it comes to your faith can be super fulfilling. Your friendships will easily move to the next level when you share a love for God.

what girls are looking for in a guy

Girls are looking for a number of things when it comes to moving a friendship to a dating relationship. Mostly, girls are looking for a guy to love them. And that's it. I've mentioned it before – girls are looking for a guy who loves and accepts them just as they are. However, we do put you into a number of categories and through a series of tests to find out if you are the one for us.

39. We make some assumptions about who you are **before we know you.**

Girls have many different categories that they put guys in to pre-determine if a guy is their type. However, type can easily be thrown out the window if we find out you like us.

Categories of Guys:
- Sweet, cute guy (girls think you are adorable)
- Smoking hot guy (girls like to stare at you and dream about your wedding)

- Super friendly and sort of cute guy (girls really like to be around you)
- Great sense of humor guy (girls have fun with you – but wonder if you can be serious)
- Super smart guy (girls like you – but wonder if you are able to loosen up and have fun)
- Artsy guy/Musician guy (girls are not sure where they stand with you; typically your music or art comes first and girls are second, and they don't really like that)
- Super athletic guy (girls like to watch you in action – being with you helps their status)
- The everything guy (you are scary for girls – you might not get a date because you are so intimidating)
- The bad boy (girls are oddly attracted to you – even though you get in trouble a lot and will get them in trouble, too)

Even though these are some of the categories that girls put you in, just be you. Don't try to fit in to a certain "type" or "category" for a girl. The list above may be how we pre-judge you, but ultimately it doesn't have much to do with the guy we decide to date. We want to date someone who is confident in who God created him to be. Your looks and our attraction level are factors, but those things become less important once we get to know you.

40. Girls are looking for a guy that takes it slow.

A girl doesn't always want to move at lightning speed. She is not looking for a guy that just wants to make out with her. She is looking for a relationship. A girl wants to get to know you and spend time with you. She wants your relationship to grow over time.

comment from kurt

Guys, girls will almost always follow your lead. It's up to you to decide you want your relationship to be a healthy, God-honoring one. Pressuring a girl physically is NEVER the right thing to do.

41. Girls want to date a guy who thinks she is the prettiest girl in the world.

Every girl wants to feel beautiful. A girl wants to date a guy who thinks she is the only girl in the world for him. A girl wants to feel attractive and beautiful to the guy she is going out with.

42. Girls are looking for someone to love them, not date them.

There is nothing casual about dating for girls. Girls are looking for love. They are looking for a relationship.

43. Girls who love God are looking for guys who love God.

Girls that are striving to follow God are looking for godly guys. Guys who know who they are and what they believe. And guys that are not afraid to show that side.

There are things you should know before you ask a girl out. You may think you are just asking a girl out for a date, but really there are a series of things to think through before you take that step.

44. Do not ask her out in front of others.

Yikes! You could possibly put both of you in an impossible situation if you do that. She might say yes, but she might say no. You need to give her the freedom to do either without embarrassing her or you in front of friends. Ask her out in private. Trust me, it's for the best.

45. Fantasy VS. Reality

Some girls are looking for a "fantasy" relationship instead of the real thing. You can blame TV and movies for this one. The media creates a "relationship fantasy world" that girls are exposed to every day. Perfect guys, in perfect scenarios, driving perfect cars, making perfect romantic gestures, all while wearing armor and riding around on a horse. Girls sometimes form their relationship expectations from the things they see in this fantasy world. Not all girls, but some. Just a heads-up; you could ask a girl out who has unrealistic expectations of you.

46. Don't **act dumb**.

Girls want to date a guy with a little smarts. Good looks could probably get you a first date – but not a second one. Girls want to date guys they can have a conversation with and enjoy hanging out with. You don't have to be making straight A's, and you can still be funny – just don't act like a dummy.

47. If you like a girl, **tell her.**

Girls like a guy with a little confidence. Games can be cute for a while, but eventually girls just want to know if you like them or not. Just save you both some time and tell her you are into her. *P.S. If she doesn't like you back or she rejects you (another reason why you don't ask her out in front of others), move on. Girls don't like it when a guy hangs on for too long.*

48. Think about dating a girl **you actually like being around.**

You might be attracted to a girl because of her looks, but think about asking a girl out that you actually have fun with. Asking a girl out just because of the way she looks might be okay for a first date, but if you can't stand her personality, it probably won't turn into a second date. If you look to date someone who is already a friend you will probably enjoy it more.

49. Don't let your friends talk you into **asking a girl out.**

You can't win in this situation. If you aren't ready to ask a girl out, then don't. You and the girl could wind up in an awkward relationship or worse – you could both end up hurt.

P.S. A girl never wants to hear that your friends prompted you to ask her out – boo you.

50. Try not to act like **you are awesome.**

It is a turnoff for girls to go out with someone who loves himself more than anything else.

comment from kurt

Ummm…but what if we **are** awesome?

51. Don't **compare us to girls** on TV or girls in movies.

We are already really critical of ourselves. The last thing we need is to be compared to someone who is impossible to live up to. *P.S. Those girls are not real. Figure this out now, or you'll be unhappy and unfulfilled your whole life. P.P.S. Lara Croft isn't real, either.*

52. Don't make assumptions about **who we are based on our personality.**

Just because a girl is quiet or reserved doesn't mean she is snobby. Her personality just might be a little more reserved than others. She could be a super fun girl once you get to know her. The quiet ones get overlooked sometimes, or because quieter girls don't have everything out in the open, guys might think they are exclusive or a snob. Not true: Shy girls have a lot to offer. But they are not going to give you the same signs as more outgoing girls.

53. Look for a girl who loves God with her whole heart.

This girl is a keeper. If you can find a girl who understands the way God loves her, then she has a great capacity and understanding for love. If she can receive God's love and pour that into others, she is worth dating.

comment from kurt

#53 Circle it, highlight it, cut it out, and paste it on your mirror. Carve it in the tree outside your bedroom window. Do whatever it takes to remember this one.

54. Look for a girl who likes you for you.

Be on the lookout for a girl who likes you for who you are — someone who does not try to change everything about you. God made you to be unique and amazing. Know that about yourself and find a girl who appreciates who God made you to be.

you're actually dating a girl

So, you got past asking her out – now what? Hanging out with a girl one on one is a huge deal. There are certain expectations and factors you need to be aware of before you knock on the front door.

55. Be a gentleman.

Open doors, pay for the date, let her enter a room first, serve her. Girls like to be taken care of on a date.

56. Think ahead.

When you ask a girl out on a date – create a game plan. Plan out where you are going to go, how you are going to get there, and what you are going to do when you get there. Girls will like that you have made the extra effort to plan something special for them. And her parents will love to hear that you have a plan for taking out their daughter for the evening. Make sure you get her home on time ... or 10 minutes early even.

57. Smell good.

Girls love a guy that smells good. But be careful – too much Axe is totally lame and smells like barf. Be subtle. Side note: This has been referenced before in this book, but it is important enough to say twice: *Seriously, take a shower.*

comment from kurt

Bummer.

58. Make eye contact.

Look your date in the eyes. It can be annoying to have a conversation with you while you are looking down at the ground or over at another table or worse, spacing out, and staring at nothing. *P.S. Try not to stare at her chest or any other body part for lingering amounts of time. She will catch you and possibly think you are a pervert.*

59. Don't be a showoff.

You already have her on a date – you don't need to get her attention. So steer clear of jumping off things, eating gross stuff, flexing, showcasing bodily functions, etc. Have fun – but don't go overboard trying to impress her by showing off.

60. Girls like compliments.

There is nothing that can start your date off right better than a compliment at the front door. When you first meet up with your date, comment on what she is wearing, how she smells, or how her hair looks. An honest compliment can keep a girl smiling for a good portion of your date.

61. Ask "interest" type questions.

Be interested in who your date is. Ask her deeper questions than, "Who do you have for math?" or "What did you eat for lunch today?" Ask her questions that will help you get to know her better. She will really appreciate that you care about knowing her on a deeper level. It will also give her questions to ask you back and get to know you as well.

Here are a few to get you started:

- What is your family like?
- How did you meet your best friend?
- What is your biggest fear?
- What drives you crazy?

62. Ask "follow-up" questions to those "interest" questions.

If you make it to a second date remember to follow up on the questions you asked in the previous date. Did she tell you something about her family? Did she talk about her friends? Did she talk about anything coming up soon in her life? Girls love a thoughtful guy who remembers what they talk about. What little cues did she send that you should remember? Less body spray on your second date?

63. Talk about you.

You don't want to seem self-absorbed but keep the conversation balanced. She will love talking about herself and she will love that you are interested in her. But she will also love getting to know stuff about you.

64. Girls might say they like surprises – but they really don't like surprises.

Girls love surprises when it comes to a present or a fun gesture, but not when it comes to a date. They want to be fully prepared for what is happening on your date. Be sure to communicate location, possible activities, and your food choice. All of these elements play into the outfit we choose, the way we do our hair, and whether or not we need a certain jacket and accessories. Be very careful when planning a surprise outing. Most girls want to be prepared, so give her something to go on so she can at least plan her outfit.

65. Do not talk about **previous girlfriends.**

Girls already compare themselves to everyone; they don't need you rubbing a past girlfriend in their face, even unintentionally. The more you talk about other girls the more insecure she will become about measuring up to those girls. And an insecure girl on a date is no fun.

66. Don't put any pressure on you OR her when it comes to **physical affection.**

Be careful when it comes to physical affection on a date. Some girls are not ready to hug, hold hands, or kiss. I think there are times when guys and girls feel the pressure to go farther physically than they want to. Alleviate that pressure by taking it slow. You don't need to hold hands or kiss to communicate how much you like someone.

comment from kurt

Guys, this might hurt a little, but here it is: If you are only interested in dating a girl because of her looks, then you aren't ready to start dating.

you're actually dating a girl

67. Follow God's example.

God is the expert on love. Let your relationship with God "leak" into your dating relationship. Loving God with your whole heart and knowing how to receive His love will help you turn around and love a girl the same way. See her the way God sees her. Treat her with respect and kindness. And show the same love to her that God shows to you.

> ### i know my gender can be confusing at times...just go with it

I am not sure how many times or how many different ways I can tell you that we are always going to keep you guessing. And there are things about us that just can't be explained.

68. The phrase "I'm fine" could be the most confusing answer a girl gives you.

The answer of "I'm fine" has many hidden meanings in girl language. When you ask a girl how she is doing and she answers with "I'm fine," it doesn't necessarily mean she is fine. It could mean that she is sad and just covering that up. It could mean that she has had a bad day. It could mean that she really is fine. It could also mean that she is just giving you a pat answer because she doesn't want to talk to you. There are many meanings behind such a simple word. You

29

can try to figure out what is behind her "fine" – but there is really no guarantee where that will lead you. Just go with it.

69. Confused? Try paying attention to our **tone of voice or our facial expressions.**

If you find yourself in a confusing conversation with a girl, you can learn a lot about how she feels by watching her facial expressions and listening to her tone of voice. You might see something on her face or listen to the way she is talking that does not match up with the actual words coming out of her mouth. This gets confusing because you are hearing one thing but getting a different response from her face or her tone of voice. Key things in this area include rolling the eyes, a hard sigh, a nervous laugh, a defensive look, tears in her eyes – and the list goes on and on. The key is to pay attention to the tone of her voice and the expression on her face. Those two things will tell you how a girl really feels even if she is saying something different...just go with it.

70. Girls like to **change the subject.**

When a girl is in a conversation that makes her feel uncomfortable in any way, she tends to change the topic of conversation. Girls hate awkward moments in conversations. So, if she can avoid that by changing the subject, she will do it in a heartbeat.

For example: Boy: "Do you have a crush on John?" Girl: "What did you get on your English test? I thought it was super hard – but I bet you did really well because you are so smart." Do you see what she did there? Not only did she change the subject when asked an uncomfortable question – but she also gave you a compliment to get you thinking about how great you are in English.

30

Sneaky, right? Girls are masters at this. We do this to keep ourselves from revealing too much to you. Just go with it.

71. Sometimes a girl just needs to cry it out.

If you see a girl crying, just be there for her. It is simply humiliating to cry in front of a guy (especially a guy that is a friend or a crush). Girls don't like to do it. Try to make it as painless as possible for her. Don't stare at her. Don't offer up any advice unless she asks for it. Don't make us feel lame for crying about something. Find one of our girl friends to hug us...just go with it.

72. Girls are fickle with likes and dislikes.

Sometimes we like something one day and don't like the exact same thing the next day. Don't ask why; that is just the way it is...just go with it.

73. Girls are very fickle with their friendships.

I would love to tell you that girls believe in "friends forever," but we don't. We can be friends with someone one day and then a situation arises between us and then we are not friends the next day. Don't ask. You can't fix it and you can't change it. And your opinion on the situation doesn't matter. We like to resolve our own friendship issues because they usually come with conditions; just ride it out and try not to take sides...just go with it.

74. Girls analyze **everything you say.**

Girls listen to what you say and then proceed to pick apart what they think you meant. If it's in writing, it gets even worse. We'll analyze handwriting, and how the note was delivered to us. We'll count the number of smilies in the text. Even if you say exactly what you mean, girls are constantly looking for a hidden meaning or agenda in your words. They analyze your tone of voice, your facial expressions, and the content of your sentence. And ultimately they come up with a conclusion for why you said what you said. Confusing, right? I know it's weird but girls rarely take what you say at face value...just go with it.

75. We can go from 0 to irrational in a **matter of seconds.**

This can be in any situation: talking about an issue, a certain person, the way you have done something annoying, a joke gone bad. We have the ability to be very irrational in any given situation. It just takes a second to flip our switch from normal to irrational. Just go with it – we will settle down eventually... just go with it.

76. If a girl is acting weird or overly emotional there is **a deeper issue.**

Things going on at home, a fight with a friend, a bad grade, a bad hair/outfit day, or an embarrassing moment can significantly alter how we move through our day and interact with others. Who we are for real – as much as we try to hide it – really affects the person you see on the surface.

i know my gender can be confusing at times

Sometimes you need to cut us some slack because we might really be hurting. The tough part is navigating our emotions and our weirdness. Sorry, there is probably nothing you can do...just go with it.

comment from kurt

Guys, I've learned that instead of trying to push for some sort of answer to why she's feeling the way she is, the best thing to do is just say something like this: "If you ever feel like talking a little more about this, I'd love to listen."

77. Every girl feels the pressure of "I'm not enough."

This can get confusing because this is an internal issue for most girls. Typically it is not related to any one situation, but a collection of situations that make them feel this way. Girls might think, "I'm not pretty enough," "I'm not smart enough," "I'm not musical enough," "I'm not popular enough" – and the list goes on. When girls get caught in the "I'm not enough" funk, there is not much you can do. You can give compliments and you can give evidence for why they are wrong, but they don't always believe you. Like I said this can be connected to any number of things. Be there as a friend to listen and encourage her. Side note: If you are the reason – say you're sorry and mean it. Just go with it.

i apologize for my gender... because girls can be mean

There is a saying that describes girls as "sugar and spice and everything nice." Have you ever heard it? It applies some of the time to girls. The other times – well, sorry, that saying couldn't be farther from the truth.

78. Girls are really competitive.

Because girls often compare, they find themselves competing with others. And at times we can take things to the extreme or do just about anything we can to be on top or be the best. Try not to get in the way.

comment from kurt

Guys, we are competitive, too, but it looks different for girls. Guys like to make bets or challenge each other in some way. Girls are usually competing for attention, social status, the affection of a guy, etc.

79. Girls like to get their way.

Yep – they do. They like it when things go according to their plan. And they really can't understand it when you don't agree or you don't see things as they do. And there are times when they can become angry with you when you don't see things their way. And there are times when they might not speak to you when you don't see things their way. Don't give in. They are not always right – they just always want to be right.

80. Girls **love to be in control.**

Girls are thinkers and planners by nature. In light of this, they really like to plan ahead and be in control of as many scenarios as possible in a day. And sometimes that control can get out of control and affect others.

81. Don't underestimate how **sneaky girls can be.**

Girls are notorious for manipulating a situation to come out in their favor. When they are not feeling good about who they are or what is going on in their lives, they will plot, scheme, connive, lie, and do just about anything to come out of a situation looking shiny.

82. Girls will do just about **anything to win a fight.**

If you get into an altercation with a girl, look out. She is going to do everything possible to win. She will humiliate you, belittle you, make fun of you, and she might even make it look like you are being mean to her. And if you are in public, beware, because she would rather die than lose face in front of friends. A girl's true nastiness can come out in a public fight.

83. Our loyalty **has limits.**

Girls can be very loyal friends – until you betray them, humiliate them, or embarrass them in front of others. At that point a girl's loyalty may have limitations. Girls can abandon a lifelong friendship in the matter of minutes if they have been wronged in any way.

84. Girls and gossip **go together** naturally.

They get super excited to pass on a good, juicy story with their closest girl friends. And sometimes they get super excited to pass on gossip to people they don't even know! They are eager to spread the nastiest of rumors and the funniest stories – the juicier the story, the better. There is actually a thrill in it for most girls. No matter who gets hurt or who the gossip is about, most girls will spread it to at least three people. And even though there are girls out there who recognize that gossip is not a healthy thing, they still do it. I know – yuck.

85. Girls think they are **smarter than you.**

We do. It doesn't matter how smart you actually are – we think we're smarter. And we will argue with you until you die to prove that we are (even if we know we are wrong). And we can get really mean in a battle of the smarts. If we don't know something, we will just cut you down to save ourselves from being embarrassed.

comment from kurt

I've been married a long time and have a teenage daughter. My wife and daughter are both way, way smarter than me – and they know it! At least, that's what I let them think.

86. Girls are **mean to one another.**

If you read the first part of this section you should already have an understanding of this one. The one thing that has not been said yet is that girls tend to be the meanest to those they are the closest to. For some reason, girls will be horrible to their best friend but extremely nice to a perfect stranger, sometimes within a sentence of another. When girls are in their comfort zone with friends, they sometimes unleash their nasty side.

87. Girls will try to use their affections as leverage **to get what they want.**

There are times when girls will use flirting as a tool to get what they want. They might act like they like you or they want to spend time with you – but they really have alterior motives. If a girl is flirting with you out of the blue, she wants something. Girls don't flirt for no reason; they flirt because they like you or they flirt because they want something or they want you to do something for them or they want to create some jealousy to get the attention of someone else. There are times when girls will do just about anything to get what they want – even if that means you get hurt or used in the process.

88. Typically, conflict is not handled **in the "nice way."**

Girls tend to deal with conflict in a different way depending on the situation. They might write you a note, they might confront you in front of others, they might give you the silent treatment, or they might tell everyone about the conflict except for the person involved.

Girls dealing with conflict usually produces drama or hurt feelings somewhere in the process.

caution: girl warnings ahead

89. Caution: Limit the gross stuff you do in front of her.

Belching, farting, and other gross bodily functions might not be the key to convincing a girl she should hang out with you. You really walk a fine line exposing this side of yourself to a girl. Some girls might think it is funny – but some girls think it's gross and they might not want to hang around you.

90. Caution: Alone time.

If a girl wants to spend a ton of alone time with you, watch out - she probably likes you (more than a friend). If you don't like her in return, you might need to draw some boundaries in your friendship and suggest hanging out in a group. Or be honest with her and let her know GENTLY that you like being friends with her and only friends. Do not LEAD A GIRL ON. It is more hurtful than you can imagine. She will make sure you carry the "player" label for a long time.

91. Caution: Hurt feelings

Girls get their feelings hurt really easily. They might put on a brave face in front of you or other friends, but as we've already established, underneath it all, girls are sensitive. If you hurt a girl's feelings and she actually tells you or you find out about it, apologize. Just say you're sorry – it will mean the world to her.

92. Caution: Jokes gone **too far.**

If you are joking around with a girl and she tells you to stop, stop immediately or she will think you are making fun of her. Most girls love to laugh and joke – but they do not like to be embarrassed or made fun of. Not all girls have the same sense of humor that you do. Nor do they totally get "guy" humor.

93. Caution: Don't be mean **to her girl friends.**

Even though girls are in competition with their best girl friends, they still listen to everything their friends have to say. If a girl's best friend thinks you are a jerk, that opinion will heavily weigh into whether or not a girl will like you. A girl's circle of friends is one of the biggest influencers in her life. Girls like to be around guys who treat their friends well.

94. Caution: Do not talk about a girl **behind her back.**

Unless you are complimenting the heck out of her, keep your thoughts to yourself. If you tease or joke about a girl behind her back, someone will tell her and she will think you are a jerk. And she will find out.

95. Caution: Do not laugh at a girl unless she **says something funny.**

When a girl sees someone laughing at her when no jokes

have been told, she instantly becomes embarrassed and insecure. If we see someone laughing at us we automatically think something is wrong.

96. Caution: Certain things **should never be mentioned.**

Never ever ever tease a girl about her weight, her appearance, or her family. She has no sense of humor about these things. Side note: *You might overhear the girl joking in these areas. Resist! It's a trap! You can't win!*

comment from kurt

Trust me fellas, this is a lesson you really don't want to learn the hard way.

97. Caution: Joking around with your guy friends **around a girl.**

You can get pretty brave when you are in your comfort zone and around your closest guy pals. The possibility for you to say something perverted or lame is high. Just enter into this situation cautiously. If you do say something lame in this situation find the girl afterward and say you're sorry.

98. Caution: Breaking **a girl's heart.**

If you are going to break a girl's heart – hmmm, not sure what to tell you in this situation. Every girl is different. Some girls will cry, some will try to hurt you back, some will try to taint your name among friends, and some will try to get all of your mutual friends on her side. It can get ugly. But if you know you don't like her, do not lead her on – break it off. Just be ready for whatever her response may be.

99. Caution: Girls don't always understand the message their appearance sends – but **sometimes they do.**

You can interpret a lot from the way a girl dresses. And there are times when girls don't understand what kind of message they are sending you through what they are wearing. There are two categories of girls in this situation. There are girls who love fashion and they love to wear what is the latest trend, whether it is skimpy or conservative – they just love clothes.

Then there are girls who are very aware of the way they dress, and they are dressing skimpy to get your attention. Showing cleavage, skimpy clothes, clothes that accentuate the positive – they wear it all so you will sit up and take notice. It can be confusing for you because you are very visual and the way we look can really heat you up. Just be cautious of the girls who are dressing solely for your benefit; there are some deeper issues there that explain why they dress that way. Something is missing in these girls; there is a reason why they use their bodies to gain acceptance from you, and it is not healthy.

last thoughts...

Girls are great – but there are other things to focus your time on.

Relationships with girls can be super fun and fulfilling. However, your relationship with Jesus Christ should take total priority in your life. If you can figure out how to follow Christ daily and live for Him, your life will be abundant beyond measure.

Enjoy the mystery!

You'll never completely figure girls out, and that's a good thing! Every girl is a little bit different, and that's a good thing, too! The world of girls will always be a bit of a mystery to you. And, yes, that's a good thing, too.

comment from kurt

My prayer for you is that you will continue to seek answers to your questions – that you will talk to your parents, to your youth pastor, and to other people you trust.

The guy/girl thing is way too important and way too difficult to navigate on your own.

I'm proud of you for taking the time to read this little book, and I hope it was a great first step in learning more about girls.

God bless!

notes